# THE LEVIATHAN'S LEGACY

# PROLOGUE

"The Leviathan's Legacy" In a world after a great disaster, people need the help of huge sea creatures created through genetic engineering. A young engineer named Gabriel discovers a conspiracy that could be dangerous for his floating island and the survival of humanity. The story begins with this mystery and promises an exciting adventure.

.

# CONTENTS

# Chapter 1
# The Mysteries of Aeropolis

The sound of the murmur of the ocean surrounding Aeropolis was the first thing Gabriel heard when he awoke. He opened his eyes slowly, allowing his senses to adjust to the glow of dawn filtering through the wide panes of his house. The view was breathtaking, with the sea's horizon stretching as far as the eye could see, unfolding an endless expanse of blue waters and clear skies. Gabriel's home, the majestic floating city of Aeropolis, stood at the center of this oceanic vastness like a fortress in the sky.

The giant towers of Aeropolis, which stood on floating platforms, towered imposingly into the sky. However, what was most striking were not the towers, but the gigantic creatures that protected the city: the Leviathans. These massive beings were a mixture of advanced technology and genetic changes, and they played a critical role in humanity's survival in a world that had experienced a catastrophe of apocalyptic proportions.

The towers of Aerópolis towered on the horizon, defying gravity while standing on floating platforms. They were real skyscrapers that seemed to touch the sky with their peaks. But what really overwhelmed those who saw them were the Leviathans, amazing and enormous creatures that silently guarded the city. These extraordinary beings were the result of a mixture of advanced technology and genetic modifications, and played a vital role in the survival of humanity in a world that had suffered an apocalyptic catastrophe of epic proportions.

Ever since he was a child, he always dreamed of working as an engineer at the Leviathan Research Unit. Every day, as he went into his work, he found himself immersed in the amazing work of studying and caring for these formidable creatures. For him, this occupation was not simply a job, but the fulfillment of a longing he had harbored since his childhood.

Their daily tasks consisted of a number of fascinating activities, such as closely observing the Leviathans, understanding their behavior, and maintaining their

well-being. This daily routine was an opportunity to continuously learn and discover the secrets of these majestic creatures. Every day at the Leviathan Research Unit was a constant reminder of humanity's ability to adapt and thrive in an ever-changing world.

Working in this environment gave him a sense of purpose and meaning, as it directly contributed to humanity's survival in a post-apocalyptic world. Every breakthrough and discovery I made as an engineer had a direct impact on preserving the human species and creating a more hopeful future in the midst of the challenges the world presented. His job was not just a career, but a passion that inspired him day in and day out.

Gabriel woke up early in his modest room in Aeropolis, the majestic floating city that rose in the sky.

It was a daily routine that I loved: waking up and approaching the large window that offered a breathtaking view of the immensity of the world suspended in the air. There, in front of that window, I could watch as the Leviathans, gigantic creatures that were the result of the union of advanced biotechnology and genetic manipulation, glided gracefully and powerfully beneath the city.

The Leviathans, in addition to being monstrous in size, were the fruit of humanity's most advanced engineering. That unique combination of biotechnology and genetics had made them much more than mere beasts. They were the undisputed guardians of the floating city, responsible for providing the essential resources necessary for humanity's survival in a world that had experienced a catastrophe of apocalyptic proportions.

On that particular morning, however, as Gabriel was watching one of the Leviathans, his gaze struck something unusual, something out of the ordinary.

In the colossal creature's behavior, he sensed a subtle change, a deviation in its movement pattern that he couldn't ignore. This anomaly, like a glimmer on the horizon, attracted his attention and filled him with a mixture of curiosity and concern.

It was as if the Leviathans, those majestic creations of science and biotechnology, were hiding secrets and mysteries that were about to be revealed. Gabriel knew in his heart that that day would mark a before and after in his life. The seed of restlessness and the need to discover the truth had been planted in his mind, and he was ready to embark on a journey full of enigmas and adventures to unravel the mysteries surrounding the creatures that sustained humanity's existence.

The Leviathan that caught Gabriel's attention at that particular moment was a towering creature. His skin had a deep blue color, which made him stand out from the rest. The creature's fins were majestic and unfolded with impressive grace as it glided through the water. This vision sounded like something out of a fairy tale, but what really caught Gabriel's attention was the unusual behavior of this colossal Leviathan.

Throughout his years of study and observation, Gabriel had come to know the movement patterns of these sea creatures with astonishing accuracy. Every movement, every turn, every breath of the Leviathans was meticulously recorded in their notebooks. But on that day, the Leviathan in question was moving in a way that defied its previous records.

Instead of the usual more energetic and rapid movements, this Leviathan moved with a slowness that was intriguing. Its fins, normally used to propel itself with force, moved slowly, and its body glided through the water with an almost hypnotic elegance. This change in his behavior was a mystery that could not be overlooked.

The deep blue Leviathan, with its unusual movement pattern, became a floating enigma in front of Gabriel's eyes. It was as if the creature was trying to communicate something, or perhaps hiding a secret beneath its majestic appearance. This discovery marked the beginning of a search for answers and adventures, a quest that would lead Gabriel to explore the mysteries hidden behind the guardians of the ocean and unravel the secrets that threatened to upset the balance in his world.

Curiosity gripped Gabriel like a burning flame within him. At the time, as he watched the deep blue Leviathan and its unusual behavior, he asked himself again and again, "What could be causing this anomaly in the Leviathan's behavior?" That question had become an enigma, a mystery that drove him to seek answers.In his mind, the intrigue began to grow like a germinating seed.

It was a sense of urgency, a kind of inner calling that drove him to unveil the truth behind this unexpected shift in the Leviathan. He could not simply turn his back on what he had witnessed; the mystery surrounding the Leviathans had caught him in his net and would not let go easily.

Gabriel knew that this day would mark the beginning of an epic quest. A quest that would take him beyond the azure waters and plunge him into the deepest secrets of Aerópolis and its gigantic sea guardians.

He was willing to brave the unknown and face the dangers that lurked on the horizon, all in his search for truth and in his determination to unravel the mysteries of the Leviathans.

Gabriel, feeling a mixture of excitement and determination, hurriedly dressed in appropriate clothes. I knew I needed to take action and address this unsettling mystery without delay.

With each piece of clothing she put on, her mind became more focused on the task ahead.

Then, with a quick but determined step, he began his descent through the intricate corridors of the floating city of Aerópolis. The corridors of the metropolis were built from an impressive combination of glass and steel, and every step he took echoed off the polished floor. As he walked through these corridors lit by the soft light of dawn, he waved his hand to his colleagues and friends.

In the heart of Aerópolis, the Leviathan Research Unit awaited, a center of knowledge and discovery that never ceased to amaze him. In those corridors, scientists and experts immersed themselves in the exploration of the colossal creatures, each dedicated to unraveling a particular aspect of the biotechnology and genetics of the Leviathans.

The looks of his colleagues were a mixture of curiosity and anticipation, they knew something important was afoot.

And although they were all immersed in their own tasks related to the study of the creatures, the spirit of collaboration and mutual support filled the air. It was a constant reminder of humanity's ability to adapt and survive in a world that had experienced apocalyptic catastrophe.

Gabriel shared with them a sense of purpose, an unwavering determination to understand the Leviathans and their importance in the post-apocalyptic world. The scientific community at Aerópolis was united in its quest for knowledge and in its struggle for survival. And on that particular day, Gabriel was embarking on a quest that would take him beyond the limits of his knowledge and plunge him into a sea of uncertainty and discovery.

Upon entering the Leviathan Research Unit, Gabriel felt a surge of excitement and anxiety. He knew that the key to understanding the anomaly in the Leviathan's behavior was buried in the records he had kept for years.

The vast archive of data was spread across shelves filled with meticulously organized notebooks, each filled with detailed observations and drawings documenting the behavior of the majestic creatures.

Carefully, Gabriel selected one of the notebooks, the one containing the most recent observations on the Leviathan in question. The pages were filled with handwritten notes and sketches of the creature swimming in its usual patterns. They were records that represented years of dedication and study. What intrigued him most, however, was the annotation on the page that morning.

In front of the window, Gabriel had witnessed something unusual, something that defied his previous records. As I flipped through the pages, I observed his meticulous notes on the normal behavior of the Leviathan in question. For years, he had come to know the movement patterns of these creatures with astonishing accuracy. But that day, his notebook showed an entry that stood out for its difference.

Instead of following its typical swimming pattern, the Leviathan in question moved in a way that had never been documented. Their movements were deliberate and slow, a dance of elegance that contrasted with the previously observed routine. Gabriel couldn't help but feel a tingle of intrigue coursing down his spine as he gazed at those notes. The anomaly in the Leviathan's behavior stood out clearly in the midst of the pages full of regular data.

Gabriel's curiosity grew as he continued to review his records. The facts were unmistakable: on that particular day, something had changed in the world of the

Leviathans. The question that consumed him was: why? What could be causing this anomaly in the behavior of one of the creatures he had studied for so long? His mind was buzzing with questions, and the sense of urgency to discover the truth behind this unexpected change was gripping him.

As
the
hours

ticked by, Gabriel dove deeper into the study of the Leviathan in question. His workbench was covered with readings, graphs, and annotations detailing every aspect of the creature's behavior. Each line and number represented a piece of the puzzle, a clue that would bring him one step closer to understanding what was happening.

Urgency and determination drove his work. Gabriel couldn't help but feel that this event transcended the mere fact of a behavioral anomaly. Every hint, every change in the Leviathan's movement pattern, filled him with intrigue and conviction that there was something deeper behind it all. More and more, he was determined to uncover the truth behind the mysterious alteration in the majestic creature's movement pattern.

Inside the quiet study room, time seemed to stand still as Gabriel delved into the records of his observations. Every detail became a piece of the puzzle I was trying to put together.

His dedication and patience were remarkable, and as he progressed in his investigation, he knew he was closer to unraveling the mystery surrounding the Leviathans.

As Gabriel progressed in his investigation, his mind was filled with questions and conjectures. Each new piece of information he collected brought him one step closer to the answer he craved. He wondered if the alteration in the behavior of the Leviathan could be due to side effects of the genetic manipulation that had given rise to these magnificent creatures. Or perhaps, he felt, there was an unknown environmental factor influencing their behavior, a mystery lurking in the depths of the ocean.

These questions became the engine of his research and the beacon that guided him in his search. With each passing day, Gabriel became more immersed in a world of mystery and wonder, where each answer found only generated new unknowns.

Humanity's survival hung in the balance, and he was aware that unraveling this enigma was crucial to understanding the delicate balance of life in Aerópolis and its uncertain future.

The answers to the questions that tormented Gabriel seemed to be just a step away, almost within his reach. Every piece of information collected, every clue discovered, brought him closer to the truth he longed to reveal. But, like a looming shadow on the horizon, a much darker mystery loomed, a conspiracy lurking in the deepest corners of Aerópolis that threatened both the floating city and the majestic Leviathans.

# Chapter 2

# The Secret of the Leviathans

After the unusual sighting of that mysterious Leviathan, Gabriel immersed himself in his investigative work, every day, heading to the Leviathan Research Unit, he felt the urgency to solve the mystery surrounding these majestic creatures.

At the core of the research unit lay an array of advanced computers, sophisticated scientific instruments, and an extensive archive of meticulously documented studies spanning several years. Gabriel immersed himself in the intricate world of data, spending countless hours analyzing observation camera footage, scrutinizing sensor measurements, and decoding the nuanced behavior patterns exhibited by the Leviathans. Each piece of information, no matter how seemingly insignificant, held the potential to unravel the mysteries that enveloped these colossal sea creatures, transforming the pursuit of understanding into a meticulous and dedicated quest.

As Gabriel delved further into Sophia's extensive research, a keen eye revealed subtle yet significant patterns in the behavior of the Leviathans, patterns that had eluded earlier observations.

The variations, though understated, recurred across different instances, sparking a realization in Gabriel's inquisitive mind. It dawned on him that these behavioral shifts weren't mere anomalies; they were, in fact, intricate clues beckoning him towards a profound and concealed reality.

One fateful afternoon, amid the dusty pages of the floating city library, Gabriel stumbled upon a document that would act as the linchpin in redirecting the trajectory of his investigation.

The parchment was worn by time and its letters were barely legible, but the contents were intriguing. It was a manuscript from a time before the catastrophe that had plunged the world into darkness.

The ancient manuscript revealed a fascinating story that went beyond anything Gabriel could have ever imagined. On its worn pages, a tale was drawn that shed light on the enigma of the Leviathans and their connection to a civilization that had existed long before the cataclysm that had ravaged the world.

The ancient manuscript unfolded a remarkable narrative, painting a picture of the Leviathans that surpassed Gabriel's wildest imaginings. According to its timeworn pages, these colossal beings were not simply products of bioengineering; they were ancient inhabitants of the Earth, entwined in a symbiotic dance with a pre-apocalyptic civilization.

This interdependence, a harmonious alliance, had withstood the tests of time, enduring through the eons. The Leviathans emerged not only as awe-inspiring sea giants but also as revered guardians and deities, occupying a divine status in the eyes of humanity. Their sacred duty was to oversee the protection and equilibrium of the world, a role that transcended the ordinary boundaries of existence.

The revelation that the Leviathans had been regarded as guardians and gods filled Gabriel with awe and wonder. It was as if he were discovering a lost part of human history, a history that had faded into the mists of time and been forgotten in the post-cataclysm era.

According to the manuscript, humanity had coexisted in harmony with these majestic beings, harnessing their gifts and abilities to thrive in a world that was kept in perfect balance.

The image forming in Gabriel's mind was of a world in which humanity and the Leviathans shared a relationship of deep respect and cooperation. The Leviathans were seen as protectors of the seas, ensuring the abundance of marine resources that sustained the pre-apocalyptic civilization. In return, mankind honored these gigantic beings and strove to preserve harmony with nature.

The revelation of this ancient symbiotic relationship had the power to change the perception of the Leviathans.

They were no longer just creations of modern bioengineering, but beings that had existed on Earth long before the catastrophe changed everything. They were guardians and gods of a forgotten age, witnesses of a humanity that had known coexistence in balance with nature.

The manuscript raised intriguing questions in Gabriel's mind. How had this ancient knowledge been lost? Why had humanity forgotten its history and its relationship with the Leviathans? Could this discovery shed light on how humanity might regain its footing in a post-apocalyptic world?

Gabriel knew he needed to share this information with his colleagues in the Leviathan Research Unit. The manuscript could hold essential clues to understanding the true nature of the Leviathans and the relationship humanity had with them in the distant past. The story unfolding before him was full of mystery and meaning, and could lead them to a new understanding of the giants of the sea.

The impact of the information Gabriel had unearthed through the ancient manuscript was astounding. If what the yellowed, history-filled pages revealed was true, then the Leviathans were not merely the result of modern science and genetic engineering, but beings who had roots that stretched back to Earth's time immemorial.

The notion that the Leviathans were not human creations, but ancestral beings who had shared Earth with ancient civilizations, resonated in Gabriel's mind as a symphony of mystery and wonder. It opened a window into a narrative that transcended modern human history and delved into the darkness of times past.

Gabriel was at the epicenter of a revelation that had the power to change the understanding of the Leviathans and, therefore, the relationship between humanity and these majestic creatures.

The pillars of his knowledge tottered, and a new image formed in his mind, an image that embraced the concept that the Leviathans were ancestral guardians of Earth, beings who had existed long before humanity developed its advanced genetic engineering.

The revelation sparked an inundation of inquiries within Gabriel's inquisitive mind. He found himself delving into a cascade of ponderings: How had the intricate bond between humanity and the Leviathans unfolded throughout the passage of centuries?

What significant roles had these majestic creatures played in the tapestry of ancient civilizations? And, perhaps most intriguingly, was there a discernible connection between the Leviathans of antiquity and their contemporary counterparts, the colossal beings that still roamed the depths of the sea? Each query unfurled like an unexplored chapter, beckoning him to traverse the corridors of time and unearth the secrets concealed within the annals of history.

The mysterious connection between the Leviathans and past civilizations became a maze of unanswered questions, and Gabriel felt like an archaeologist of humanity's hidden history. Every page of the manuscript was a puzzle, and he was willing to fit each piece together to reveal the full picture.

The discovery of the manuscript had opened a new chapter in Gabriel's research.

The possibility that the Leviathans were part of a symbiotic relationship with ancient civilizations opened up a range of perspectives and challenges that inspired him.

The evidence pointed to the catastrophe that ravaged the Earth and plunged humanity into despair was intrinsically linked to the Leviathans. Something had happened, something that had led to  the creation of the floating city of Aeropolis and the genetic manipulation of these creatures. But what had caused the breakdown of harmony between humans and the Leviathans?

Determined to solve this riddle, Gabriel embarked on a search for additional information. He consulted ancient records, maps, and stories that had survived the passage of centuries. Each new clue brought him closer to understanding the relationship between the Leviathans and the catastrophe that had marked the world.

As he progressed in his research, his mind was filled with images of a forgotten past: Leviathans swimming in the clear seas, ancient civilizations worshipping them as divinities, and the harmony that had once reigned on Earth.

However, he also glimpsed the shadows of a conflict, a traumatic event that had led to the creation of the floating city and the sacrifice of nature in favor of humanity's survival.

 Gabriel was not alone in his search. He shared his discoveries with his friend and fellow scientist, Sophia. Together, they analyzed ancient documents and collected evidence, and began to tie up loose ends. Their collaboration became essential, as the two investigators realized they were uncovering a truth that had been hidden for far too long.

As they delved deeper into the history of the Leviathans and their relationship to the catastrophe, they also encountered those who preferred these secrets to remain buried.

The floating city of Aeropolis, which once seemed like a safe haven, was becoming a dangerous place for Gabriel and Sophia. The warnings and threats multiplied as they continued to dig into the history of the Leviathans and their connection to the catastrophe.

The pair of scientists were in the midst of a much bigger conflict than they had imagined, and they were determined to get to the bottom of the truth, no matter the consequences.

# Chapter 3

# The Conspiracy Uncovered

Intrigued by his findings, Gabriel felt the need to share his research with his Sophia. As they pieced together the puzzle, they discovered evidence that clearly pointed to the existence of a conspiracy unfolding in the shadows of Aeropolis. The conspirators seemed determined to take control of the Leviathans, the gigantic sea creatures, and use them for occult and dark purposes.

Gabriel decided to invite Sophia to his house that afternoon. When she entered her home, she was amazed by the abundant light that flowed through the glass that surrounded the room. Radiant particles of sunshine lit up every corner, and the atmosphere was imbued with a sense of warmth and mystery.

The room was designed with a clear purpose: the investigation of the Leviathans. A sturdy and solid table was located in one of the corners of the room, and was crammed with documents, ancient manuscripts, and detailed observation records about the majestic sea creatures.

Gabriel prided himself on his extensive collection of information, and every handwritten page or photocopy held an important place in his quest to decipher the mysteries of the Leviathans.

The walls were lined with meticulous diagrams detailing the anatomy and behavior of the Leviathans, along with photographs that captured their grandeur and majesty. Each image featured these creatures in their natural habitat, gliding through the abysmal depths, surrounded by the vastness of the ocean. The sea creatures stared with curious eyes from the images, and Gabriel and Sophia could feel their presence through the images around them.

The room was a sanctuary dedicated to the research and admiration of the Leviathans. Gabriel's passion for these creatures was clear in every corner, and Sophia couldn't help but be captivated by the aura of mystery and wonder that filled the room. It was a place where science and art met.

As Gabriel shared his findings and discoveries with Sophia, his passion and enthusiasm overflowed. Every page of his manuscripts and every detailed observation he had recorded was a window into an uncharted world, and he was eager to share it with someone who could appreciate his work and understand his dedication. Together, they explored the mysteries of the Leviathans, and time seemed to stand still in that sunlit corner, where science and wonder intertwined in a dance of discovery and wonder.

Gabriel began to recount his findings, as he spoke, he pointed to the ancient manuscripts he had found in the floating city's library. Sophia listened intently, and as Gabriel continued, they began to notice patterns emerging in the information. The Leviathans, once regarded as guardians and gods, had been an integral part of an ancient civilization that had coexisted with them in harmony. These giants of the sea were not just creatures created by science, but beings that had existed on Earth since time immemorial.

This knowledge raised new questions and possibilities that they had not yet fully considered.

"It's as if they were guardians of the Earth," Sophia said, "they provided resources, they maintained ecological balance, and the ancients revered them as divinities. But something changed. Something that led to the creation of Aeropolis and the sacrifice of nature in favor of the survival of humanity."

His investigation began to focus on uncovering the threads of this conspiracy. Together, they reviewed communications logs, interrogated other scientists, and looked for connections between the influential individuals who ruled Aeropolis. What they discovered was unsettling and terrifying. There was a secret group of powerful people who were interested in taking control of the Leviathans and using their immense power for purposes that escaped them.

As they delved deeper into the investigation, they realized they were entering dangerous territory.

Warnings and threats began to pile up, they had crossed a line, and those who would prefer these secrets to remain buried were unwilling to allow their discoveries to spread.

Chapter 4:

# The Riddle of the Abyss

Determined to get more answers about the origin and purpose of the Leviathans, Gabriel was faced with a bold and risky decision. He felt that the key to uncovering the mysteries of these majestic creatures and their connection to pre-apocalyptic civilization and the catastrophe that had ravaged the world lay in the depths of the ocean. With this resolution, he made up his mind to embark on a journey that would take him into unknown and dangerous territory.

Gabriel embarked on a quest that would lead him to the unfathomable depths of the ocean, where he believed priceless secrets were hidden. He knew this journey was fraught with risks and challenges, but the urgency of truth propelled him forward. Armed with a state-of-the-art research submarine, he set out from Aerópolis for an unknown world, a realm of vastness and darkness that stretched beyond the floating city.

Venturing further into the profound depths of the ocean, Gabriel found himself enveloped in an increasing shroud of darkness, as if the very essence of mystery and isolation clung to the aquatic expanse.

Even with the cutting-edge technology embedded in his submarine, the ocean retained its enigmatic allure, an expansive realm teeming with secrets and perils that eluded the grasp of human understanding. The abyssal journey became a dance with the unknown, where each submerged moment held the potential for unveiling the ancient riddles concealed within the watery embrace of the deep.

As Gabriel descended into the profound realms of the ocean, he embarked on a journey of exploration, delving into the remnants of shipwrecks and the echoes of an ancient civilization. Among the algae-covered structures adorned with coral, he encountered the silent testimony of a bygone era, a time when Leviathans and humans shared the world in harmonious coexistence.

Amidst the underwater ruins, veiled in the passage of time, Gabriel unraveled clues that hinted at a connection between humanity and the colossal beings that surpassed even his wildest imagination. The submerged artifacts became portals to a forgotten era, whispering tales of a symbiotic alliance that transcended the boundaries of mere existence.

The ancient remnants that Gabriel meticulously investigated were adorned with captivating inscriptions and mysterious murals, each stroke of the artwork telling a tale of a distant past. These archaeological treasures unveiled the narrative of a bygone golden age, a time when Leviathans commanded admiration as unparalleled guardians and divine entities of the vast seas. The inscriptions etched into the stones and the enigmatic depictions on the murals painted a vivid picture of a forgotten era where these colossal beings held a revered status, their presence synonymous with protection and divine order in the aquatic realm.

The ancient inhabitants of Earth revered these colossal creatures with deep respect and regarded them as divine figures who ruled the oceans.

Legends passed down through the generations recounted how the Leviathans were the purveyors of life, responsible for maintaining the ecological balance of the vast oceans. They were much more than just sea creatures; They were the backbone of the pre-apocalyptic civilization that had faded over the centuries. Their symbiotic relationship with humanity was the core and soul of that society, an ancestral pact between two worlds that coexisted in harmony.

The Leviathans, with their power and majesty, provided essential resources for the subsistence of coastal communities. Their flesh nourished populations, their fins provided valuable materials, and their movements regulated the natural cycles of the seas. These extraordinary creatures were the guardians of the ocean's wealth, ensuring the survival of humanity.

Their sea gods were depicted in the murals in stunning detail, each scale and fin reverently recreated.

Inscriptions on the walls of the ruins told stories of rituals and ceremonies dedicated to these colossal beings, and how their blessings were critical to the prosperity and balance of the world.

The story that emerged from the murals and inscriptions spoke of a time of symbiosis and respect, where humanity had learned to coexist in harmony with nature and its marine guardians.

The discovery of this ancient civilization and its relationship to the Leviathans raised new questions. What was the meaning of this symbiosis? What secrets were hidden in ancient rituals and ceremonies? Could these ancient teachings shed light on the mystery behind the recent alteration in the behavior of the Leviathans? Gabriel was faced with an ancient enigma.

As Gabriel deepened his investigations, he unearthed damning evidence of a catastrophe that had relentlessly shaken the ancient civilization, marking a break in the harmony that had once reigned.

The traces of this disaster became visible throughout his explorations, manifesting themselves in the form of ruins of cities submerged in the abyssal depths. These ancient metropolises, now reclaimed by the waters, were silent testimonies to the heartbreaking impact that had devastated society at the time.

Not only had cities been engulfed by the waters, but shipwrecks of ancient ships lay strewn across the seabed, distressing reminders of the despair and chaos that had prevailed in the midst of catastrophe. Gabriel could almost feel the intensity of the conflict and the desperate struggle for survival that had taken place in that tumultuous period.

Devastation spread like a dark cloak, shrouding these ruins and shipwrecks in an aura of sadness and sacrifice, where humanity had faced colossal challenges in a desperate attempt to survive the fury of catastrophe. Each of Gabriel's finds shed new light on the tragic events that had sparked an age of darkness.

As Gabriel delved deeper into the mysteries of the abyss, a complex puzzle began to form in his thoughts. The clues and evidence he uncovered painted a compelling picture of how the cataclysmic event had triggered a chain of events, ultimately leading to the genesis of the floating city of

Aeropolis and the genetic engineering of the Leviathans.

The calamity had forced humanity into a corner, pushing them to take unprecedented measures for survival. In this dire context, the Leviathans emerged as not just majestic creatures of the sea but as indispensable components of a survival strategy.

Within the depths of the ocean, Gabriel stumbled upon an ancient structure, a sanctum that seemed to serve as a sacred tribute to the Leviathans. The walls of this underwater shrine were adorned with intricate inscriptions and detailed reliefs that narrated the profound tale of the symbiotic connection between the ancient civilization and these colossal sea creatures.

As Gabriel delved deeper into the sanctuary, the depictions on the walls unfolded intricate scenes of elaborate ceremonies and offerings, all infused with an undeniable atmosphere of reverence and respect for the majestic Leviathans. The very essence of the shrine seemed to echo with the deep connection that the ancient civilization had shared with these sea giants, portraying them not just as guardians but almost as divine beings.

While examining the inscriptions within the sacred space, Gabriel's attention was drawn to a series of ancient writings that hinted at a prophecy entwined with the Leviathans and their purpose in times yet to come. These inscriptions, weathered by the currents of time, sparked curiosity within Gabriel, urging him to unravel the secrets concealed within the prophetic words etched on the sacred walls.

This prophecy spoke of a time when the Leviathans would once again play a crucial role in the fate of humanity.

The revelation of this prophecy left Gabriel astonished and bewildered. Could it be that the Leviathans had a deeper purpose and a closer connection to the catastrophe than they had imagined? The truth was beginning to emerge, but questions remained unanswered.

As Gabriel emerged from the mysterious depths of the ocean, safely returning to the confines of his submarine, a profound reflection washed over him. The wealth of discoveries beneath the waves had unveiled a narrative far more intricate than he had initially perceived. The evidence pointed to the Leviathans transcending their status as mere bioengineered entities, revealing them as ancient beings intricately entwined with humanity in a symbiotic dance that spanned the epochs of time.

The cataclysmic event had irrevocably shifted the dynamics of this age-old relationship, leaving Gabriel to grapple with the implications of a bond disrupted by the dark machinations of conspirators.

It became increasingly apparent that these colossal sea creatures were not only pivotal to the survival of humanity in the distant past but were now being manipulated for ominous and occult purposes by those with nefarious intentions.

The riddle of the abyss lay before him, but Gabriel knew he was closer to uncovering the truth behind the sea colossi and the catastrophe that had ravaged the world.

# Chapter 5

# Unexpected Allies

As Gabriel ventured deeper and deeper into the depths of the sea abyss, he came across a group of daring sea treasure hunters. Even though their goals were different, there was a tacit acknowledgment between them. It was the determination to uncover the mysteries of the Leviathans that brought them together in this dark underwater realm.

The meeting took place in the twilight of the abyss, where sunlight barely penetrated. Gabriel had been exploring the marine world, analyzing ancient shipwrecks and submerged ruins, when he came across the crew of the treasure hunter ship. These intrepid adventurers had ventured into the depths in search of valuables that had lain hidden for centuries.

The leader of the underwater expedition, a man by the name of Leon, stepped forward towards Gabriel, a curious glint in his eyes. "What brings you to these profound depths?" he inquired, his voice resonating in the watery surroundings.

In response, Gabriel unfolded his quest for understanding, delving into the mysteries of the Leviathans and their intricate ties to an ancient civilization. He unraveled the tale of the colossal sea colossi and their role in the catastrophic events that had reshaped the very fabric of the world. As he spoke, the gravity of his words hung in the underwater atmosphere, creating a sense of shared intrigue among the expedition members.

As he spoke, he noticed the spark of interest in the eyes of the treasure hunters. While their goal was to find valuables, the idea of uncovering the mysteries of the Leviathans also captivated them.

The group of treasure hunters consisted of a variety of individuals with diverse and complementary skills. There were expert divers who knew the secrets of the seafloor, engineers who had modified their equipment to operate in the depths, and cartographers who drew detailed maps of the areas explored.

The diversity of skills became an invaluable asset as they began to collaborate. Gabriel brought his scientific knowledge to the table, allowing for a deeper understanding of the evidence and findings related to the Leviathans. Treasure hunters, on the other hand, contributed their expertise in searching for valuable objects on the seabed, which proved to be useful in uncovering the secrets hidden beneath the deep waters.

As they went on their quest, their unexpected alliance grew stronger. Together, they braved dangerous ocean currents, unknown sea creatures, and the overwhelming darkness of the abyss. Gabriel's fiery determination merged with the bravery of the treasure hunters, creating a team spirit that propelled them forward.

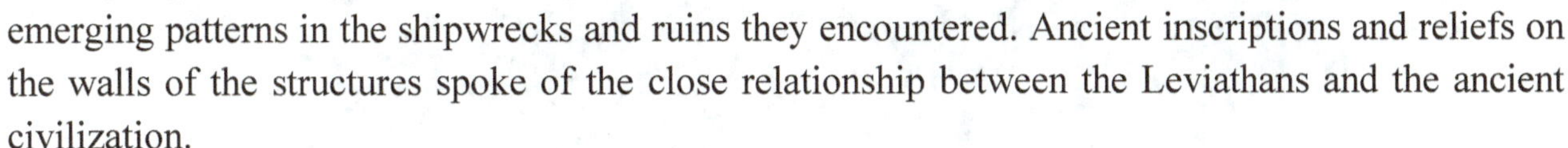

As they explored deeper, Gabriel began to notice emerging patterns in the shipwrecks and ruins they encountered. Ancient inscriptions and reliefs on the walls of the structures spoke of the close relationship between the Leviathans and the ancient civilization.

There were images of ceremonies and offerings that suggested that the ancients revered these colossal creatures and depended on them for their survival.

 The revelation of this ancient connection between the Leviathans and humanity stunned Gabriel. It was clear that the Leviathans were not simply bioengineered creations, but ancestral beings that had existed on Earth since time immemorial.

The catastrophe had disrupted this symbiotic relationship and led to the creation of Aeropolis and the genetic manipulation of the Leviathans.

Collaboration with treasure hunters became essential as they faced obstacles in their quest. Together, they came up with ingenious solutions to get around the odds and continue exploring the depths of

the ocean. As they made their way deeper into the sea abyss, they came across evidence that suggested an ancient prophecy related to the Leviathans and their role in the future.

The ancient prophecy unfolded a narrative that foretold a future where the Leviathans would reclaim their pivotal role in shaping the destiny of humanity. It painted a vivid picture of a time when the immense power of these sea giants would become indispensable in the task of reinstating equilibrium to a world that had been fractured by a cataclysmic event.

The prophecy whispered of an era where the Leviathans, majestic beings with a history intertwined with that of humanity, would emerge as the beacon of hope and restoration.

Their significance in the cosmic symphony of nature and human existence was destined to resurface, guiding the way toward a harmonious coexistence between mankind and the forces of the natural world.

The revelation added a new level of mystery to their quest. Gabriel realized that they were closer to discovering the truth behind the Leviathans and their role in the catastrophe that had ravaged the world.

Collaboration with treasure hunters had not only provided them with valuable skills and resources, but also a sense of unity in their unwavering pursuit of truth.

# Chapter 6

# The Oracle of the Ocean

The quest for knowledge led the team to explore an ancient shipwreck, a relic submerged in time. Tension filled the air as they descended into the depths of the ocean, illuminated by the lights of their submarines. The darkness of the sea abyss seemed eternal.

Inside the wreck, they found a mysterious artifact lying in a dark corner. This artifact glowed with a faint glow and was covered in ancient symbols and cryptic inscriptions. Gabriel's heart pounded as he examined it closely. He had found something truly extraordinary.

As the team gathered around the artifact, a tense silence descended upon them. It seemed that the artifact had a kind of consciousness of its own. Then, suddenly, it was activated. Flashes of light spread from its surface, illuminating the darkness of the wreck. The glow of the ancient symbols came to life and they began to move, forming words and phrases in an ancient language that resonated in their minds.

He foretold the fate of the Leviathans and their connection to the catastrophe that had ravaged Earth. It mentioned a legendary being known as the Oracle of the Ocean, an ancient entity who possessed profound knowledge about the Leviathans and the catastrophe that had shaped the world.

The prophecy unveiled a cryptic message: "In the deepest shadows beneath the waves, the Oracle of the Ocean patiently resides. Holder of age-old mysteries, it safeguards the truth. The Leviathans, beings woven into the fabric of both science and history, bear a connection to the fate of humanity. Only through the Oracle's guidance can the intricate threads of their role in calamity and renewal be unraveled. Venture into the profound abyss, and therein lies the key to the answers your heart yearns for."

The discovery sent shockwaves through the team, their collective astonishment echoing in the dimly lit space.

The prophecy, a beacon of insight, indicated the existence of a being possessing unparalleled wisdom—the Oracle of the Ocean. This revelation acted as a catalyst, igniting a fervent desire within the team to embark on a quest in search of this enigmatic figure. Their sense of purpose deepened, fueled by a newfound determination to uncover the secrets entwining the Leviathans and the ancient mysteries of the deep sea.

They understood that the answers to their fundamental questions lay in the unfathomable depths of the sea abyss.

The artifact, with its flashes of light and prophecy, provided them with a clear path and direction to follow. Their search was filled with a new sense of urgency. The evidence and revelations they had uncovered so far had brought them to a point of no return, and they were willing to face any challenge in their search for the Oracle of the Ocean.

As they descended deeper into the sea abyss, the world around them became stranger and more mysterious. Unknown sea creatures passed by, and the ocean currents took on an unpredictable intensity. They were in uncharted and dangerous territory, but nothing could stop them.

The team relied on the diverse skills and experience of its members. Treasure hunters brought their knowledge in navigation and underwater exploration, while Gabriel provided his scientific understanding and passion for discovering the truth.

# Chapter 7

# The Journey to the Deep

The team ventured further into the sea abyss, braving the unknown depths as they approached the place where the Oracle of the Ocean was believed to reside. Every kilometer descended into the abyssal depths led them to an even more enigmatic and mysterious realm.

The ocean abyss unfolded like a captivating story of wonder and intrigue. With each descent, Gabriel and his team found themselves immersed in a mesmerizing realm beneath the waves. The coral reefs, adorned with a kaleidoscope of hues, unveiled a hidden tapestry of underwater marvels. A vibrant mosaic of shapes and colors painted a scene that transcended the boundaries of imagination. Exotic fish, with their peculiar forms, gracefully navigated the depths, while bioluminescent creatures cast a celestial glow, turning the darkness into a magical spectacle. The journey into the sea's depths became a symphony of beauty and mystery, captivating the explorers at every turn.Despite the impending dangers, the beauty of the abyssal depths took their breath away. It was a constant reminder of the wonder and majesty of the underwater world, a world few had had the privilege of exploring.

The underwater currents became more and more treacherous as they descended deeper. In this hostile environment, the team had to be on constant alert, using their skills and experience to navigate the troubled waters. The currents could change direction in an instant, dragging them into the unknown and testing their ability to stay the course.

The sea creatures they encountered on their journey were equally astonishing and enigmatic. Some were nightmarish creatures with twisted appendage s and glowing eyes, while others were graceful beings that glided through the darkness with hypnotic elegance. Each encounter was a showcase of

the diversity and complexity of the underwater world, and added an extra layer of mystery to their journey.

As they progressed, the team realized that they were approaching the place where the Oracle of the Ocean was believed to dwell. The prophecy had provided them with clear direction, and they were determined to follow the path that lay before them.

Their fiery determination drove them, and their insatiable curiosity kept them alert to every sign, every revelation that might bring them closer to their goal. Despite the dangers and uncertainties they faced, Gabriel and his team were determined to keep going. The prophecy of the mysterious artifact had given them a clear purpose.

# Meeting the Oracle

After a grueling journey through the deep sea, the team finally arrived at the place believed to be home to the Oracle of the Ocean. An underwater sanctuary opened up before them, illuminated by the light of bioluminescent waters that created a spectacle of dazzling colors in the surrounding waters. It was a breathtakin g setting for his encounter with the legendary entity that had been the target of his search.

The underwater sanctuary stood as a breathtaking marvel. Towering coral pillars, adorned with a myriad of life forms, ascended gracefully from the ocean floor, displaying a mesmerizing array of dazzling colors. The bioluminescent waters exuded a gentle radiance, creating an enchanting ambiance that bathed the entire sanctuary in a magical glow. Within this ethereal setting, exotic sea creatures moved with a captivating grace, their movements enhancing the feeling that the sanctuary itself pulsed with life and vibrancy.

Each corner of this submerged haven held a spectacle of beauty, a testament to the wonders hidden beneath the ocean's surface.

At last, the Oracle revealed its presence to the team. Emerging from the depths of the ocean with awe-inspiring majesty, it commanded attention with its imposing size. Its eyes, mirrors of ancient wisdom, conveyed a profound understanding that seemed to transcend the passage of countless ages. The sheer grandeur of the Oracle's appearance left the team in a state of wonder, as they marveled at the magnificent being that stood before them, a living testament to the ocean's secrets.

The creature appeared to be an ancient being, exuding an aura of authority that permeated the entire sanctuary. Its venerable presence commanded a mixture of respect and trepidation, as it became evident that the team was in the company of an extraordinary and otherworldly entity.

The air was thick with a sense of reverence, as the team grappled with the realization that they were in the presence of a being that transcended the ordinary boundaries of time and understanding.

The Oracle communicated with a resounding voice that resonated within their minds, eliminating the necessity for spoken words. "You have ventured here in pursuit of answers and wisdom," it conveyed, "and indeed, you find yourself in the correct realm. However, knowledge is not without its costs. Everything exacts a toll." The profound message hung in the air, emphasizing the profound truth that the acquisition of wisdom often requires sacrifices or trade-offs.

Demand sent a chill down the team's spine. They realized that they wouldn't get answers without first offering something in return. Tension rose as they considered the implications of their encounter with the Oracle.

He demanded a tribute, an act of sacrifice that would demonstrate his commitment to the pursuit of knowledge. Each member of the team was faced with a personal challenge, a choice that would influence the course of their lives.

As the forefront figure of the team, Gabriel found himself at the forefront of the Oracle's trial. The Oracle posed a profound challenge to him: relinquish his role and existence in Aeropolis, plunge into the profound depths of the sea, and establish a life in harmony with the Leviathans.

The Oracle disclosed that Gabriel held the potential to evolve into the intermediary connecting humanity with these majestic sea beings—a role crucial to maintaining equilibrium in the world. The proposition laid before Gabriel was not merely a request; it was an invitation to embark on a transformative journey that could reshape the course of his life and humanity's destiny.

In Sophia's case, Gabriel's scientific comrade, a distinct set of options presented themselves. He was extended an invitation to delve into the depths of bioengineering science, unraveling th e enigmatic workings of the Leviathans. Yet, this journey came at the cost of forsaking the comforts of surface life and immersing himself in the solitude of an underwater laboratory. The prospect opened a door to unparalleled knowledge, but it demanded a sacrifice—trading the bustling surface world for the solitary confines of the abyss. It was a proposition that weighed the allure of scientific revelation against the solitude of underwater exploration.

The treasure hunters faced their own set of dilemmas. The Oracle posed a question that demanded a departure from their lucrative pursuits in exchange for a higher calling – safeguarding the profound mysteries of the deep sea and ensuring the well-being of the Leviathans.

This trade-off involved relinquishing the exhilarating pursuit of valuable artifacts in favor of embracing a life steeped in dedication and sacrifice. The call to protect the ocean's secrets and uphold the delicate balance with the Leviathans required a profound shift in their priorities, asking them to exchange the thrill of material gain for a deeper, more profound sense of purpose.

# Chapter 9

# The Pact with the Deep

Gabriel and his team had faced the challenge of the Oracle of the Ocean, and after deep reflection, they had decided to accept the proposed pact. The burning determination to uncover the truth behind the Leviathans and the conspiracy that threatened Aeropolis drove them to sacrifice much for this cause. They were ready to seal the pact with the Oracle and bear the consequences of their choice.

The underwater sanctuary was filled with a mixture of emotions as they prepared to accept the pact. The excitement of finally getting answers to their questions was intertwined with apprehension about the uncertain future that awaited them. They knew that they were on the threshold of a significant change in their lives and that the covenant they were about to seal would have profound implications.

The Oracle, with its imposing presence, watched them with wise eyes. He didn't need words to communicate with them, as their connection was deep and telepathic.

Gabriel wholeheartedly embraced the covenant laid before him, displaying a profound readiness to forsake the familiarity of his life above the surface and plunge into the profound depths of the sea. In doing so, he willingly assumed the pivotal role of mediator, serving as a connective link between the realm of humanity and the enigmatic Leviathans—an endeavor aimed at reuniting two worlds that had, for far too long, existed in isolation.

Their collective dedication, he understood, held the key to sustaining the delicate equilibrium that governed the world.

Sophia, the scientific companion of Gabriel, wholeheartedly embraced the terms of the agreement as well. She demonstrated an unwavering commitment to relinquishing her existence on the surface, opting instead for a life of solitude within the confines of an underwater laboratory. In this secluded environment, she dedicated herself to the profound exploration of Leviathans and the intricate field of bioengineering.

Initially hesitant, the treasure hunters, captivated by the profound significance of the pact, eventually embraced their designated role. They willingly cast aside their pursuits of treasure hunting, choosing instead to embark on a transformative journey as guardians of the deep sea and the Leviathans. Their wealth of knowledge and expertise in underwater navigation emerged as crucial assets, ensuring the safety and well-being of these majestic beings in their newly bestowed role.

Once the pact was sealed, a wave of energy swept through the underwater sanctuary. It was as if the world itself recognized his commitment and determination. The Oracle nodded in approval, and his voice echoed in their minds: "You have made a brave and sacrificial decision. The knowledge you seek will be yours, but it also comes with great responsibility."

With the pact sealed, the team prepared to return to Aeropolis. They had new information and a renewed perspective on the Leviathans and the conspiracy that threatened them.

They understood that their return would be the beginning of a decisive confrontation against the occult forces that sought to control the Leviathans and, through them, the fate of Aerópolis.

# Chapter 10
## Dark Secrets Revealed

Back in Aerópolis, Gabriel and his team found themselves faced with the arduous task of sharing the findings obtained in the deep sea with the authorities and exposing the web of conspiracy that extended to the highest levels of society.

This was a monumental challenge, as treachery and danger lurked in every corner of the majestic floating city. The conspirators were determined to protect their secrets and were willing to go to any lengths to maintain their control.

The tension in Aeropolis increased with each passing day. Gabriel  and his allies had returned with information that would shake the foundations of the floating city and expose the conspiracy that had brewed in the shadows. The gravity of the situation did not go unnoticed, and they soon realized that they would face fierce resistance from those who wished to keep their interests hidden.

The team began sharing their findings with the Aerópolis authorities. They presented irrefutable evidence of the existence of  a conspiracy that aimed to take control of the Leviathans for dark and unknown purposes. The faces of the city's leaders reflected surprise and concern as they understood the magnitude of the threat looming over them.

However, the revelation of the conspiracy also provoked a backlash from the conspirators. Soon, Gabriel and his allies found themselves in the crosshairs of those who were willing to eliminate any threat to their interests. Betrayal and danger became an everyday part of their lives, and they had to be on constant alert to protect themselves and the information they had discovered.

The threats they faced were diverse and constantly lurking around every corner. Gabriel and his team had to deal with a series of problems that had become part of their daily routine.

Tempting bribes, espionage attempts, and acts of sabotage had become constant shadows hanging over them. Simply trusting those around them became an uncertain dilemma, as they couldn't be sure who they could really trust. The web of conspiracy they had unearthed had been skillfully woven into every level of Aerópolis society, further complicating their quest for truth and justice.

Every day was a battle for integrity and bravery as they faced these insidious threats. Tempting offers of bribes tested their loyalty and commitment to their cause. Attempts at espionage, designed to undermine their efforts and keep secrets hidden, required constant vigilance and the protection of the valuable information they had gathered. The sabotage, on the other hand, directly threatened the security of his research and, ultimately, the safety of the Leviathans and Aerópolis as a whole.

Uncertainty about the loyalty of those around them hung like a constant shadow.

They did not know if a trusted friend had been influenced or coerced by the conspirators, leading to tensions and doubts in their inner circle. Bonds that were once solid became fragile, and betrayal loomed as a constant threat in their struggle for truth.

The vastness of the conspiracy, with its tentacles reaching into every corner of Aeropolis society, made the struggle for truth and justice even more intricate. The conspirators' connections extended to influential and powerful figures in the floating city, allowing them to weave a web of complicity that made it increasingly difficult to unravel the threads of their plot.

The magnitude of the threat impelled them to be even more resolute in their search, knowing that the truth was their best weapon against this conspiracy in the shadows.Despite the dangers they faced, Gabriel and his team did not back down.

With the support of brave individuals in Aerópolis who had recognized the veracity of the evidence presented, Gabriel and his team began the process of creating a clandestine resistance.

This network of secret allies, like unsung heroes, operated in the shadows, committed to exposing the conspiracy and protecting those who dared to confront it. Their struggle to uncover the truth turned into intense combat, and the floating city of Aerópolis became the scene of an epic conflict that had the potential to rewrite the fate of all involved. The brave individuals who joined the underground resistance did so driven by deep conviction and a sense of justice. They had seen the evidence Gabriel and his team had collected, and they were willing to risk their own lives to defend the truth and fight the conspiracy that threatened Aeripolis and the Leviathans. These brave allies operated in the shadows, avoiding detection by the conspirators.

The underground resistance transformed into a tightly-knit and united front against the pervasive conspiracy. Operating discreetly in the shadows, they engaged in the exchange of vital information, meticulous strategic planning, and synchronized efforts designed to unveil the conspirators and thwart their sinister designs. Motivated by an unyielding commitment to truth and justice, they found their inspiration in the pursuit of a greater cause, fearlessly confronting any peril that dared to obstruct their path.

The quest for truth evolved into an epic and intense battle, a fierce struggle that unfolded not only in the vibrant streets of Aeropolis but also within the shadowy corridors of the floating city. The stakes soared to unprecedented heights, with the destinies of the  Leviathans and humanity precariously hanging in the balance. The conspiracy, a formidable adversary, cast a pervasive shadow over the city, but the underground resistance emerged as a beacon of determination and courage.

Driven by an unwavering commitment, they were ready to deploy every conceivable effort to unravel the concealed secrets, safeguarding the floating city from the ominous uncertainties that loomed on the horizon.

# Chapter 11
# The Siege of Aerópolis

The conspirators, driven by an escalating sense of urgency, shed their cloak of secrecy and initiated a bold assault on Aeropolis, the resplendent floating city that had served as the residence of Gabriel and his steadfast allies. In a mere matter of minutes, the once serene streets of the city transformed into a frenetic battlefield, the echoes of war drowning out the once-peaceful ambiance that graced its every corner.

The clamor of conflict resonated through the atmosphere, creating a thunderous symphony that echoed across the expanse of the floating city. This tumultuous orchestra pierced the ears of the astonished citizens, who peered out from windows and balconies of their ethereal abodes, their eyes wide with terror, captivated by the harrowing spectacle unfolding below. The cityscape, once adorned with the grace and splendor characteristic of Aeropolis, now radiated a different kind of luminosity—marked by bursts of explosions and intermittent flashes casting dim, ominous lights.

This spectacle, which stood in stark contrast to the majesty of the city, represented a grim reminder of how the order and peace that had once reigned in

Aerópolis, which was once a serene haven, had undergone a stark transformation into a tumultuous battleground. The previously tranquil streets, bustling with peaceful activities, were now engulfed in the chaos of a fierce conflict between the city's inhabitants and the conspirators. The darkness of the night was pierced by frequent explosions and flashes of turmoil, serving as relentless indicators that Aerópolis teetered on the brink of peril, with the very essence of their existence hanging in the balance.

Amid the ongoing conflict, Gabriel found himself at the forefront of the defenders of the city. The preparation undertaken by their group had foreseen this critical juncture, understanding that the exposure of the conspiracy would inevitably elicit a strong and retaliatory response from the conspirators.

The anticipation of such repercussions had driven their readiness, and now, in the heat of the battle, Gabriel led the charge to safeguard the city against the impending threats.

The confrontation that unfolded in the streets of Aeropolis evolved into an intense struggle for existence, a clash where each moment presented a challenge that demanded not only courage but also unwavering determination. In this pivotal juncture, Gabriel, alongside his steadfast companions, stood at a crucial intersection, confronted by a merciless adversary. This opponent, formidable and meticulously

equipped, exhibited a relentless resolve, leaving no avenue unexplored in their pursuit of ominous objectives. The daunting nature of the opposition heightened the gravity of the situation, putting the courage and resilience of Gabriel and his allies to the ultimate test.

The streets, which had once been the scene of the daily lives of peaceful citizens, had now been transformed into a chaotic battlefield, where bursts of fire and explosions created an environment of constant danger.

The future of the floating city was in grave jeopardy, and every decision and action of Gabriel and his allies was crucial to protecting what was left of peace and stability in Aerópolis. The threat looming over the city was bigger and darker than they had ever imagined, and the struggle for truth and justice had become more intense and vital than ever.

The conspirators, fueled by relentless determination, surged forward with ferocity, employing state-of-the-art technology and ruthless strategies to achieve their sinister aims. The once serene streets of Aeropolis transformed into chaotic battlegrounds, resonating with the echoes of violent clashes.

Defenders valiantly engaged with the invaders, their every move an effort to thwart those who sought to lay claim to the Leviathans. The city itself quivered under the weight of the siege, the intensity of the struggle escalating as the battle for dominion over the colossal sea giants reached a fever pitch with each fleeting second.

As the relentless battle wore on, Gabriel and his steadfast allies came to a profound realization: they were engaged in a struggle that transcended the mere survival of Aerópolis. At the heart of their defense was a commitment to safeguarding the last beacon of hope for humanity—the Leviathans. These majestic sea creatures, carefully crafted to endure the challenges of a post-apocalyptic world, symbolized not only the survival of their floating home but also the delicate equilibrium of the entire world.

With the fate of their city and the very balance of the planet hanging in the balance, they faced the desperate battle with unwavering determination, ready to expend every ounce of effort in this crucial fight.

Moments of heroism and sacrifice followed as the defenders of Aerópolis fought valiantly to protect the Leviathans and keep the conspirators at bay. The city became a symbol of resistance, a beacon of hope in the midst of chaos.

Despite the daunting challenges, Gabriel and his allies did not back down. They knew they were striving for a purpose greater than their own lives. The battle dragged on for hours that seemed endless.

The floating city was filled with smoke and destruction, but the defenders did not surrender. Every moment of resistance was an act of bravery, a reminder that the fight for truth and justice was worth it. As the sun set over Aerópolis, the conspirators began to retreat, defeated by the determination of those who had confronted them.

# Chapter 12
# The Battle in the Heavens

Aerópolis, the floating city, entered a fresh chapter in its quest for survival. The conflict escalated to the skies, transforming into a breathtaking spectacle of aerial warfare. In this epic duel, Gabriel found himself at the helm of a powerful air combat machine, steering it with the skill and determination of a seasoned leader.

The clash unfolded as he led the charge against the conspirators who sought to dominate the Leviathans, engaging in a high-stakes battle where the fate of the floating city hung in the balance.

The night sky above Aerópolis underwent a spectacular transformation, setting the stage for an epic battle that held everyone's attention. The powerful engines of the ships roared, creating a symphony of sound that blended with the explosive thunder echoing through the air. Amidst this cacophony, the sky became a canvas illuminated by dazzling bursts of light from the explosions.

The flickering lights of projectiles and the streaks left behind by the agile fighters painted a breathtaking scene, a mesmerizing display that rivaled the natural beauty of the stars adorning the expansive celestial dome.

The skies, which had once been a place of wonder and serenity, had become a scene of heart-wrenching conflict.

Battleships sliced through the air with their breakneck speeds, maneuvering in a deadly dance as they engaged in a game of cat and mouse. Flashes and explosions lit up the darkness of the night, creating a visual spectacle that reflected the magnitude of the confrontation. The natural beauty of the stars and moon was marred by the intensity of the battle raging in the skies of the floating city. The adrenaline and tension were palpable as each pilot fought to maintain supremacy in the vast skies of Aeropolis.

Gabriel understood the gravity of the situation. At that moment, he was leading the battle in the skies, and the outcome of this confrontation would determine the fate of Aerópolis and, ultimately, all of humanity. It was a heavy burden he carried on his shoulders, but he also knew he couldn't afford to hesitate.

As the sleek air combat ships gracefully glided through the airspace above Aeropolis, Gabriel became fully engaged in a high-stakes duel that demanded both skill and strategic prowess. The conspirators, realizing the gravity of the situation, had assembled an impressive fleet of aerial warships.

The ensuing battle unfolded with an intensity that could only be described as fierce, each pilot executing daring maneuvers and employing lethal strategies in a bid to secure an advantage over their

adversaries. The clash of metal and the thunderous roar of engines echoed through the skies as the aerial ballet of combat unfolded.

Explosions lit up the sky and the roar of anti-aircraft artillery filled the air. Gabriel and his allies were facing a determined and well-trained enemy who was willing to go to any lengths to achieve their goals.

Despite the daunting challenges, Gabriel's resolve did not waver. He had gone too far in his search for the truth and was willing to give his all to protect the Leviathans and their home.

The fighting in the skies raged for hours that seemed endless. The pilots faced off in a duel that challenged the limits of endurance and skill.

The air fighters performed dizzying maneuvers, avoiding enemy shells and trying to gain the upper hand. Every moment was a reminder of the ferocity of the battle and the importance of the mission. As the night wore on, the situation became even more intense. Gabriel and his allies fought relentlessly, knowing that they were in a fight that would determine the future of Aeropolis and humanity.

The floating city represented humanity's last hope in a post-apocalyptic world, and they were willing to give their all for its survival.

The battle in the skies finally reached a critical point. Gabriel and his allies managed to gain the upper hand, forcing the conspirators to retreat. The enemy ships drifted away, defeated by the bravery and determination of those who had faced them. Aeropolis had withstood another attack, and the conspiracy was in retreat.

# Chapter 13
## Shocking Revelations

In the midst of the chaotic battle in the skies of Aeropolis, Gabriel achieved a moment of clarity that led him to unravel the truth behind the conspiracy. Through a series of discoveries and connections, he understood the pivotal role the Leviathans played in restoring balance to a world ravaged by catastrophe. Along with this revelation, however, came the knowledge of an immense sacrifice that would be necessary to accomplish it, a sacrifice that filled him with sorrow and anguish.

As the aerial battleships continued their tumultuous clashes in the starry expanse above Aeropolis, Gabriel sensed a surreal slowing of time around him. His journey had been one of relentless exploration through the city's archives, tirelessly pursuing clues, and methodically connecting the scattered pieces of the intricate puzzle. With unwavering determination, he had delved into the mysteries, and at last, the fragments coalesced into a comprehensive panorama, unveiling the truth in all its vastness before him.

As he delved deeper into his research, Gabriel made an astonishing discovery that changed his understanding of the Leviathans.

Beyond their fundamental duty as protectors and suppliers of vital resources for Aeropolis, Gabriel unearthed a profound revelation about the Leviathans.

These magnificent creatures weren't just guardians; they stood as extraordinary beings meticulously crafted through genetic engineering. Their purpose went beyond mere protection, extending to the remarkable task of absorbing and neutralizing the catastrophic aftermath of the bygone apocalyptic events. They were, in essence, living correctors of the environmental upheaval that had reshaped the world.

 The Leviathans were humanity's last hope for reversing the devastation that had plunged Earth into a state of desolation. Their existence was intricately linked to the ability to heal the wounded world. They were like beacons of hope in a world marked by devastation, able to counteract the aftermath of the apocalyptic catastrophe that had left deep scars on the Earth.

Understanding this new dimension of the Leviathans filled Gabriel with awe and a renewed urgency to protect these creatures and their vital importance to humanity's survival.

The discovery of the truth was tinged with a heart-wrenching knowledge that weighed heavily on Gabriel's heart.

Despite the vital importance of the Leviathans in restoring ecological balance, this process required sacrifice of immense proportions. The Leviathans, despite their noble function, needed a very specific type of energy to carry out their task of healing the wounded world. This unique and powerful source of

energy was located in the place the inhabitants of Aeropolis called home: the same floating city that depended on the resources of the Leviathans to survive.

The dilemma Gabriel and his team faced was heartbreaking. To heal the Earth and ensure humanity's survival, they had to sacrifice the very source of energy that sustained Aeropolis.

This act would require a delicate balance and a deep understanding of the consequences. The price of Earth's rebirth was high, and every decision they made would affect not only the Leviathans, but the floating city and all of its inhabitants.

 The emotional charge of this choice filled Gabriel with anguish, as he contemplated the uncertain future and the decisions they had to make in the name of humanity's survival.

The revelation struck Gabriel to the core of his being. He was at a crossroads, faced with a decision that would determine the fate of the Leviathans, Aeropolis, and humanity as a whole. The weight of responsibility weighed him down, and his thoughts became entangled in a storm of ethical dilemmas and mixed emotions.

The sacrifice required to use Aeropolis as a source of energy for the Leviathans was a heartbreaking and dilemma-ridden decision. It meant risking the safety of the floating city and the lives of its inhabitants, those whom Gabriel had sworn to protect.

The implications of this choice were overwhelming, as it required Gabriel to weigh the life and well-being of humanity against the possibility of restoring balance to a world that had suffered so much.

Each alternative was fraught with unfathomable consequences, and Gabriel was at a crucial turning point where he had to make a decision that would affect not only the Leviathans and Aeropolis, but the very fate of humanity. The pressure and emotional charge of this choice consumed him as he faced a decision that would redefine his legacy and the course of history.

As he contemplated his decision, Gabriel felt the pressure of the expectations of his allies and humanity as a whole. The floating city was looking to him for leadership, and his election would affect everyone. The battle in the skies and in the streets of Aerópolis continued unabated, and Gabriel knew he had no time to lose.

Finally, Gabriel made his decision. The struggle for truth and justice had brought him to this critical moment, and he knew he could not turn back.

# Chapter 14

# Gabriel's Choice

Gabriel found himself standing at a pivotal and emotionally challenging crossroads. The weight of the decision ahead of him was immense, with colossal consequences hanging in the balance. On one hand, there was the option to sacrifice the Leviathans, potentially saving humanity but at a profound cost. On the other, he could explore alternative solutions, but the risks involved were significant and the potential outcomes unknown. The burden of making a choice that would impact the lives of thousands pressed heavily on him, and the magnitude of the consequences was both daunting and overwhelming.

The weight of the decision burdened Gabriel emotionally. He was acutely aware that the very survival of humanity rested on the choice he was about to make, a choice that held the power to shape the destiny of everyone. Each option presented him with complex ethical dilemmas, intertwining fears, and aspirations.

Gabriel found himself grappling with the profound responsibility  of weighing the life and well-being of humanity against the potential for restoring balance to a world scarred by past catastrophes.

One of the options presented was to sacrifice the Leviathans, offering the promise of using their power to reverse the catastrophe that had left Earth in a state of desolation.

This choice opened up the possibility of humanity's salvation, representing a unique opportunity to restore the Earth and ensure a sustainable future for generations to come. However, this choice also came at a high price, as it would mean the loss of the Leviathans, majestic creatures that had been guardians and providers of essential resources in Aerópolis.

Gabriel was faced with a daunting dilemma, in which he had to weigh the well-being of humanity and the potential for restoration of the Earth against the sacrifice of these awesome creatures that had been central to the survival of his floating city.

The election would not only be an act of bravery, but a testament to humanity's ability to make crucial decisions at critical moments.

The other option before Gabriel was the search for an alternative solution. This choice involved risking everything in the process, as there was no certainty that a viable alternative would be available.

Despite the uncertainty, Gabriel carried with him a deep belief in the ability of human science and engineering to find innovative solutions even in the most challenging of times. He was convinced  that if they tried hard enough, they could discover a different way to restore balance to the world without having to sacrifice the Leviathans. However, this choice was also fraught with risks, as time was of the essence and there was no guarantee that a solution would be found in time. The consequence of not succeeding in this quest could be the destruction of the floating city and the survival of humanity hanging by a thread.

Gabriel found himself in an overwhelming dilemma, facing the tension between hope and uncertainty, as he contemplated an uncertain future for Aerópolis and its people.

The weight of the responsibility to determine the destiny of numerous lives, including those of the Leviathans, the city of Aeropolis, and humanity as a whole, felt like an immense burden on Gabriel's shoulders. The gravity of the situation pressed upon him, making the decision a monumental task that carried profound implications for all involved.

As he weighed the pros and cons of each option, Gabriel felt the weight of the expectations of his allies and the floating city as a  whole. The city looked to him for leadership and direction, and his election would influence the fate of all. I knew I had no time to waste and that I had to make a decision soon.

Gabriel was faced with a heartbreaking choice, and ultimately opted to seek an alternative solution rather than sacrifice the Leviathans.This choice was rooted in his deep belief in the potential of science and humanity's ability to discover innovative answers even in the most challenging of times.

For him, sacrificing the Leviathans was the last option, something he would only consider after he had exhausted all possibilities of finding an alternative to restore balance to the world. His determination and desire to preserve these majestic creatures drove him to take this uncertain and risky path.

Gabriel was willing to risk everything in hopes of finding a solution that would not involve the sacrifice of the guardians of Aerópolis while also allowing humanity to survive on a restored world.His election marked a turning point in his quest for justice and in the fight for the survival of Aeropolis and humanity. Although the future remained uncertain, he had chosen the path that he believed would lead to the best solution for everyone.

The battle for control of the Leviathans and the restoration of balance to a wounded world continued, and Gabriel was ready to face every challenge that came his way in his quest for truth and justice.

# Chapter 15

# The Sacrifice of the Leviathans

The decision Gabriel had to confront marked one of the pivotal and demanding moments in his entire existence. Following a period of profound contemplation and meticulous examination, he reached the conclusion to sacrifice the Leviathans. In doing so, he aimed to fulfill the ancient prophecy that held the promise of Earth's restoration.

The magnitude of this choice was overwhelming, and the weight of responsibility rested on his shoulders. As he prepared to unleash the necessary cataclysm that would change the course of history, Gabriel was filled with deep grief and sadness.

The decision to sacrifice the magnificent creatures, who had served as vigilant guardians of Aeropolis, weighed heavily on Gabriel's heart. He couldn't ignore the depth of the sacrifice these majestic beings were about to make for the well-being of humanity and the restoration of the world they all cherished.

The sorrow within him was profound, recognizing that the choice he had made would have far-reaching consequences, ultimately shaping the destiny of Aeropolis.

The event that unfolded was of unimaginable magnitude. The Leviathans, those majestic sea creatures that had been guardians and providers of essential resources in Aeropolis, prepared to fulfill their crucial role in the restoration of the Earth.

The forces of nature were unleashed in an apocalyptic display of power, and the resulting devastation was shocking and palpable in every way. The magnitude of the cataclysm was breathtaking, and the floating city of Aerópolis trembled under the unleashed forces. The population, filled with astonishment and sorrow, saw the magnitude of the catastrophe that was taking place before their eyes. The explosions, rumblings, and commotion created by the Leviathans marked a before and after in the history of the floating city and its role in restoring a fractured world.

The floating city of Aeropolis quivered beneath the immense forces unleashed upon it. It was rocked by mighty earthquakes that sent buildings trembling and floating platforms swaying violently. The once-stable foundations of the city were now subjected to powerful forces from below, threatening the very structure of this majestic haven in the sky.

The residents, once accustomed to serene heights, now found themselves grappling with the chaotic upheaval that shook their homes and world.

On the distant horizon, towering tsunamis surged and loomed, menacingly threatening to swallow the floating city whole. Simultaneously, volcanic eruptions violently erupted, expelling ash clouds and rivers of molten lava, transforming the Earth's surface into a catastrophic spectacle. The once picturesque vista surrounding Aeropolis was now a battleground between the elemental forces of water and fire, each vying for dominance and wreaking havoc on the serene environment that once defined the city's skyline.

The skies were filled with dazzling lightning that illuminated the darkness, accompanied by cataclysmic storms that shook the celestial vault with deafening thunder. The roar of hurricane-force winds mingled with the roar of explosions, creating natural chaos of epic proportions. The magnitude of the catastrophe was overwhelming, and the inhabitants of Aerópolis, from their floating dwellings, watched with amazement and sorrow the immensity of what was unfolding. The floating city was at the epicenter of Earth's transformation, and all its inhabitants shared the emotional charge and awe of this unprecedented event.

 Gabriel, accompanied by his team and the inhabitants of Aeropolis, watched the sacrifice of the Leviathans with a heavy heart. Tears welled up in the eyes of many, and mingled with the rain that fell on the floating city, as if heaven itself shared their sadness.

Mourning filled the streets as people gathered in silence, paying homage to these majestic creatures who had been guardians and providers of essential resources for Aerópolis for so long.

The magnitude of the Leviathans' sacrifice was evident to all. They realized that this heartbreaking act had been necessary to restore balance to the world. Although it weighed heavily on their hearts, there was also a feeling of gratitude and respect for these creatures who had given everything for the survival of humanity.

The people of Aeropolis understood that Earth's rebirth would not have been possible without the sacrifice of the Leviathans, and this generated a deep sense of responsibility and appreciation for their role in the restoration of the world.

Grief and sadness gripped the hearts of the people of Aerópolis. They had suffered irreparable losses, losing loved ones, close friends, and the city guardians who had shared their home for so long.

The magnitude of the devastation that was unleashed as a result of the sacrifice of the Leviathans was immense and poignant.

The streets of Aeropolis were filled with grief as people mourned the departure of these sea giants. The floating city, which used to be a place of joy and beauty, was plunged into an atmosphere of melancholy.

 Despite the pain that gripped the city, there was also a shared sense of hope. The inhabitants of Aerópolis knew that, through this sacrifice, the door was opened to a better future for  humanity and for the Earth. Although the sadness was overwhelming, there was also the promise of a rebirth, of an opportunity to heal the wounds of the world and restore balance to the Earth. Faith in that brighter future gave them the strength to face the difficulties of the present and work together to build a better world.

As the cataclysm subsided and the Earth began to heal, Gabriel and his team found themselves facing a whole new challenge.

Restoring the floating city and adapting to a world that had undergone such a profound transformation were monumental tasks. Despite the sadness and losses they had faced, hope shone on the horizon.

The rebuilding of Aerópolis began with a renewed sense of  togetherness and purpose. The community worked tirelessly to restore the beauty and functionality of their beloved city. Damaged buildings were repaired, streets were repaved, and gardens bloomed again. The floating city was filled with life and activity, as its inhabitants struggled to restore normalcy.

Yet, the task of reconstructing the city was only the tip of the iceberg in the myriad challenges they confronted. Beyond the boundaries of Aeropolis, a grand transformation was unfolding. The oceans, once desolate and somber, underwent a remarkable rejuvenation, teeming with vibrant marine life that danced beneath the revitalized waves. Lands that had long lain barren experienced a resurgence of life.

The skies above cleared of the lingering shadows of the past, unveiling a celestial canvas that showcased the unparalleled beauty of nature reborn on Earth.

As the inhabitants of Aerópolis adapted to this transformed world, they also struggled to heal the wounds of society that had spread during the conspiracy and battle. Trust and unity became essential to building a better future. The lesson they had learned from the

Leviathans, about the importance of coexisting in harmony with nature, became more relevant than ever.

 The restoration of balance in the world had begun, and humanity had a unique opportunity to build a more sustainable future. The catastrophe that had ravaged the Earth had been a hard lesson, but it had also been a catalyst for change. The inhabitants of Aerópolis realized that they needed to care for and protect their home, live in harmony with nature, and work together to make sure that the mistakes of the past were not repeated.

The restoration of balance in the world, marked by the sacrifice of the Leviathans, had laid the foundation for a more hopeful world. Gabriel and his team, along with all of humanity, faced a challenging future, but they were willing to build a better world, full of unity, care for nature, and hope. The lesson they had learned from the events that had brought them to this point guided them on their way forward, determined to create a world in which humanity and nature could coexist in harmony.

# Chapter **16**
# The Rebirth of the Earth

As the Earth began to heal and regain its former glory, the scars of catastrophe were still visible in every corner of the world. Gabriel and the survivors found themselves on the threshold of a new chapter of history, where they had to rebuild a new and hopeful world, facing the reality of the actions taken and the repercussions of their choice.

The landscapes that had endured the devastation were beginning to undergo a startling transformation. Nature, with its astonishing capacity for regeneration, was beginning to recover from the wounds inflicted by the catastrophe.

Where before there was only desolation and sadness, now life flourished again in every corner. In the once desolate and lifeless lands, a miraculous resurgence of nature took place. Small, tender green shoots emerged from the soil, serving as resilient symbols of hope and new beginnings.

These tiny plants courageously pushed their way through the earth, reaching towards the warm embrace of sunlight, symbolizing the unstoppable force of life returning to the previously barren terrain.

The seas, which had been exhausted and lifeless, were undergoing an equally impressive transformation. The coral reefs, once gloomy reminders of a previous world, were now teeming with life and color. Fish of all sizes and colors swam among the corals, while sea creatures filled the waters with their beauty and diversity.

The skies, once shrouded in the turmoil of cataclysmic storms, were gradually revealing a newfound clarity. The sun, with its gentle and comforting radiance, illuminated the rejuvenated Earth in a warm, golden glow. The tumultuous storm clouds that had dominated the heavens now yielded to the emergence of clear, star-studded skies, presenting a breathtaking spectacle of natural beauty that could rival the grandeur of any human-created marvel.

The transformation of the landscapes was not only a reminder of the power of nature, but also a symbol of hope. The Earth was healing, and life was regaining its place in the world. The restoration of balance, marked by the sacrifices of the Leviathans and the bravery of those who had fought for it, was bearing fruit.

A brighter, more sustainable future was on the horizon, and humanity was ready to meet the challenges ahead with renewed determination.

However, despite the beauty of Earth's rebirth, humanity was also faced with the challenge of repairing broken relationships and healing the wounds

of society that had spread during the conspiracy and battle at Aeropolis. The consequences of the actions taken and the magnitude of the Leviathans' sacrifice weighed heavily on everyone's hearts and minds.

Gabriel, as an unwitting leader in this new era, was overwhelmed by the responsibility to lead his people into a brighter future.

The choice he had made, though necessary, had left a deep impression on him. He felt the pressure to do justice to the sacrifice of the Leviathans and the hope they had placed in him.

The floating city had suffered significant damage during the battle, and a concerted effort was needed to restore it to its former glory.

The city's inhabitants worked tirelessly, united by a sense of shared purpose and a determination to build a stronger, more resilient home.

The divisions caused by the conspiracy were slowly healing, and confidence in the authorities and in society's ability to prevent future conspiracies was strengthening.

But the healing was not limited to the floating city of Aerópolis, it embraced the entire world. Nations from all corners of the globe came together in a joint effort, in an unprecedented show of solidarity, to repair the damage caused by the devastating catastrophe.

On the global stage, where leaders from various nations convened in international conferences and negotiations, extensive discussions unfolded concerning comprehensive strategies to tackle the pressing issue of climate change, safeguard delicate ecosystems, and

promote the sustainable utilization of Earth's natural resources. These diplomatic efforts resulted in the formulation of crucial international agreements, marking a pivotal step in the collective commitment to preserving the invaluable treasures of nature and averting potential catastrophes in the times to come.

Environmental awareness grew as humanity recognized the fragility of the Earth and the importance of caring for it. Conservation, reforestation and ecological restoration projects were multiplying everywhere. Scientists and experts worked tirelessly in the search for innovative solutions to environmental challenges, and environmental education became an integral part of the school curriculum around the world.

Humanity's commitment to restoring the Earth became a legacy, a promise to future generations to care for this planet and live in harmony with nature. The catastrophe that had threatened to destroy everything became a turning point, at a time when humanity came together to heal the wounds of the Earth and protect its future.

Reconciliation commissions were established and dialogue and understanding between the different factions of society were promoted. It was a long and difficult process, but the lesson learned from the conspiracy had left a deep imprint on everyone.

With the passage of time and the rhythmic cycle of seasons, the Earth embarked on a remarkable journey of renewal. Diverse ecosystems, ranging from the sprawling expanses of verdant forests to the vibrant tapestries of coral reefs beneath the ocean waves, exhibited unmistakable signs of resurgence.

The once-silent landscapes were now echoing with the sounds of diverse and vibrant life.

Wildlife, having weathered the challenges during the peak of the disaster, was reclaiming its natural habitats, meticulously restored through unwavering care and dedication. Majestic elephants roamed freely, their trumpets echoing through the renewed forests, while tiny insects diligently went about their essential roles, contributing to the symphony of life that resonated in every corner of the world.

As the dawn of a new era unfolded, humanity embraced its responsibility as

stewards of the planet. A profound shift in mindset had occurred, emphasizing the importance of environmental preservation and fostering global cooperation. In this transformed world, key decisions at both individual and collective levels were guided by a commitment to sustainability. Renewable energy emerged as the cornerstone of progress, progressively supplanting traditional fossil fuels and contributing to a substantial reduction in carbon emissions. The harmony between human life and the Earth became a guiding principle, steering the course towards a balanced and sustainable future.

In this transformed world, technology took center stage, with a dedicated focus on sustainability. Innovations emerged, revolutionizing production and consumption methods to be more efficient and environmentally conscious. A new era of mobility dawned, characterized by the widespread adoption of sustainable practices. Electric vehicles seamlessly integrated into daily life, while low-emission public transport systems became the backbone of urban commuting. Cities underwent a green makeover, adorned with lush urban green spaces and equipped with highly efficient recycling systems. The once-distant dream of harmonizing technological progress with ecological responsibility had become a tangible reality, shaping a future where humanity and the environment coexisted in a symbiotic balance.

In the united effort to combat environmental challenges, global cooperation played a pivotal role. Nations collaborated closely, pooling their resources and expertise to tackle issues such as climate change, safeguarding biodiversity, and promoting fair access to natural resources.

The bonds of international agreements and environmental treaties were fortified, reflecting a shared commitment within the global community to safeguard the beauty and balance of the natural world for the well-being of generations to come. This spirit of collaboration became the cornerstone of a sustainable future, where the nations of the world worked hand in hand to protect the planet and ensure a harmonious coexistence with nature.

The promotion of environmental education became a widespread and integral aspect of the curriculum for young minds. Schools and educational institutions championed the cause of environmental awareness, instilling in students a deep understanding of the importance of preserving nature. Reforestation programs flourished, offering individuals the chance to actively participate in the noble endeavor of protecting and restoring the environment. These initiatives not only contributed to the physical rehabilitation of ecosystems but also nurtured a sense of responsibility and care for the natural world.

Although environmental challenges continued to pose hurdles, humanity emerged from its tumultuous history with invaluable lessons. The catastrophic event, which had cast a shadow of apocalyptic proportions, served as a catalyst for a worldwide shift towards a more sustainable and responsible future. It acted as a poignant reminder of the Earth's significance as our singular home, urging collective efforts to safeguard its inherent beauty and diverse ecosystems. The trials of the past became stepping stones toward a harmonious coexistence with nature, emphasizing the profound impact that united global endeavors could have in preserving the planet for generations to come.

Gabriel's decision, though laden with pain, served as the catalyst for a fresh start. The sacrifice of the Leviathans became the cornerstone for restoring equilibrium in the world and laying the foundation for a more sustainable future. While the grief and sorrow stemming from the loss of these magnificent creatures lingered, their legacy endured in the revitalization of the Earth and the optimism for a brighter tomorrow.

The profound and lasting impact of the Leviathans' sacrifice served as a guiding light, pointing humanity toward a renewed sense of responsibility and a harmonious coexistence with the natural world. The narrative of Gabriel and his unwavering quest for truth and justice transcended mere history; it evolved into a legendary tale, forever etched in the collective memory of humanity. It stood as a powerful reminder of our inherent capacity to confront colossal challenges, overcome adversity, and strive for a better, more sustainable future. Gabriel's journey became a symbol of courage, resilience, and the enduring pursuit of a world where nature and humanity coexist in balance.

In the vibrant tapestry of Earth's rejuvenation and the dawn of a promising era for humanity, the legacy of the Leviathans and their selfless sacrifice became a timeless source of inspiration for countless generations. The tales of these majestic beings and their pivotal role in restoring the planet echoed through the corridors of time.

The memory of the Leviathans served as a beacon, guiding humanity to cherish, protect, and preserve the beauty and balance of their cherished home. The lessons learned from their sacrifice became an integral part of the collective consciousness, fostering a commitment to stewardship and ensuring that the Earth remained a haven for generations yet to come.

# Chapter 17

# The Return of the Oracle

The Oracle of the Ocean returned at a time when Gabriel and his team were still immersed in the reconstruction and reconciliation efforts at Aerópolis. News of his return quickly spread through the floating city, creating a buzz of excitement and anticipation among its inhabitants. The Oracle, with its ancient wisdom, had played a crucial role in the restoration of Earth, and its latest revelation was awaited with great interest.

The meeting with the Oracle unfolded as a majestic and ceremonial spectacle, transforming the underwater encounter into a solemn event. Gabriel, surrounded by his steadfast team, embarked on another descent into the profound depths of the sea, where the underwater sanctuary patiently awaited their arrival. The ambiance was charged with reverence as they approached the ancient creature, whose majestic presence exuded both a calming sense of peace and an undeniable air of authority. The underwater sanctuary, set the stage for a momentous communion between the inquisitive humans and the wise Oracle.

The Oracle, an ancient and wise entity, commenced communication in an archaic language that reverberated throughout the underwater chamber.

As its words echoed, a transcendent glow enveloped the surroundings, casting an ethereal luminosity that rendered Gabriel and his team momentarily speechless. The chamber, adorned with mysterious symbols and ancient inscriptions, seemed to come alive with the energy of the Oracle's ancient wisdom. The underwater sanctuary became a realm where the boundaries between the tangible and the mystical blurred, creating an awe-inspiring atmosphere that captivated the explorers.

What the Oracle shared was a vision, a picture of the future that not only stole their breath but also filled them with wonder and hope.

In the mystical vision revealed by the Oracle, Gabriel and his team witnessed a vivid portrayal of a world where the Leviathans transcended their historical roles.

The imagery painted a picture of a harmonious alliance between humanity and these sea colossi, united in a shared commitment to preserve the natural wonders of the deep blue.

The Leviathans, in their ceaseless efforts, undertook the noble task of safeguarding the richness of marine life. Their diligent work extended to preserving the diverse web of marine biodiversity, maintaining a delicate

balance within the vast ecosystems of the oceans. Every corner of the ocean, from the tiniest microscopic algae to the mightiest ocean giants, felt the positive impact of their guardianship.

The Leviathans, with their innate understanding of the interconnectedness of all species, played a vital role in preventing any one element from overpowering and disrupting the delicate harmony that defined the underwater world.

This vision of the future showed the oceans teeming with life, with vibrant coral reefs and fish of all colors plying the waters.

The Leviathans, in their collaborative efforts, formed symbiotic relationships with various sea creatures.

They generously offered shelter to sharks, creating a harmonious coexistence within the oceanic realm. Additionally, their influence extended to the regulation of jellyfish populations, ensuring a delicate balance that  supported the overall health of the underwater ecosystems.

The cooperation between these different marine species became a cornerstone for the sustainability and vitality of the intricate web of life beneath the ocean's surface.

Beyond their guardian duties, these colossal beings actively contributed to sustaining water quality. Their innate ability to filter particulate matter and purify the oceans had a profound ripple effect, positively influencing not only the marine environment but also the quality of Earth's air. The Leviathans, emerged as essential guardians, not only of the seas but also of the broader well-being of the entire planet.

This revelation from the Oracle left Gabriel and his team with a renewed sense of admiration and gratitude toward the Leviathans. Not only had these majestic sea creatures been heroes in the past, but they continued to play a critical role in the preservation and balance of the Earth. The vision of the future they had witnessed filled them with determination to protect and preserve the Leviathans.

As Gabriel and his team delved further into the revelations offered by the Oracle, the intricate ties between sea creatures, the catastrophic event, and the subsequent restoration of Earth unfolded in a way that surpassed their initial comprehension. It became increasingly clear that their journey was not solely about uncovering the mysteries of the Leviathans; it had evolved into a profound realization of the paramount importance of sustaining a harmonious balance with nature. The Oracle's visionary insights became a guiding light, illuminating the path for Gabriel's role in safeguarding the Earth.

The vision shared by the Oracle made it clear that the Leviathans had not completely disappeared from the face of the Earth, but had followed a path of evolution and adaptation. Their transformation had made them guardians of the seas, taking on a new purpose that was intrinsically linked to the preservation and balance of the marine ecosystem.

In their evolved form, the Leviathans had developed amazing abilities that allowed them to communicate in special ways with other sea creatures.

The communication among sea creatures, led by the Leviathans, went beyond the limitations of language, serving as a vital mechanism for sustaining harmony within the oceans. This intricate collaboration extended to various marine inhabitants, including dolphins, whales, sea turtles, and a diverse array of species. Through this coordination, they worked together to safeguard biodiversity, preventing any one species from exerting destructive dominance and contributing to the overall health and balance of the marine ecosystems.

In their capacity as marine guardians, the Leviathans concentrated on fostering the well-being and equilibrium of marine ecosystems. Serving as a natural regulator, these majestic beings played a crucial role in controlling the populations of specific species, thereby averting ecological imbalances. Through their unique ability to influence the distribution of marine life, the Leviathans facilitated a harmonious coexistence among various species in the vast oceans.

In addition to their role as guardians, Leviathans also played a crucial role in purifying seawater. Their massive bodies absorbed and neutralized pollutants and harmful particles, contributing significantly to maintaining water quality in the oceans. Not only did this process benefit sea creatures, but it also had a positive impact on the Earth's air quality and climate.

This new way of life of the Leviathans allowed them to continue their legacy as guardians of the Earth, ensuring that the seas remained a source of life and balance on the planet.

The Oracle's vision provided a profound insight into the evolutionary journey of the Leviathans, illustrating that while thei r physical forms had undergone transformations and adaptations, their core mission of safeguarding and preserving marine life and ecological balance remained their most sacred and enduring purpose.

The revelation of this evolution of the Leviathans left Gabriel and his team in awe of nature's ability to adapt and survive.

The Leviathans, once guardians of humanity in times of catastrophe, were now guardians of the marine world, watching over the health and harmony of the oceans. It was an impressive display of the interconnectedness of all forms of life on Earth and a lesson in the importance of respecting and protecting nature for the good of the entire planet.

The revelation profoundly impacted Gabriel and his team, providing a comprehensive understanding of the Leviathans and the significance of their sacrifice.

The realization dawned upon them that the Leviathans had transcended their initial role as colossal bioengineered beings to embrace a noble purpose as guardians of marine life and environmental stewards.

The sacrifice made by the Leviathans had not been without purpose; rather, it had laid the foundation for a world where humanity and nature coexisted in harmonious balance.

The Oracle also shared one last lesson: the importance of learning from history and not repeating the mistakes of the past. He reminded Gabriel and his team that the catastrophe had been caused in part by the uncontrolled exploitation of natural resources and a lack of regard for ecological balance. He urged them to be responsible stewards of the Earth, to preserve the beauty of the oceans, and to learn to live in harmony with nature.The final revelation of the Oracle left a deep impression on Gabriel and his team.

Gabriel and his team returned to the surface, taking the Oracle's teachings with them. They shared the revelation with the people of Aerópolis, inspiring the floating city to embark on a new era of preserving and caring for the environment.

# Chapter 18

# Epilogue: The Legacy of Aeropolis

The city of Aeropolis, which had endured devastation from both conspiracy and intense battles that posed a threat to its existence, was undergoing a remarkable phase of renewal and recovery. The residents of this floating city joined forces in a united endeavor to reconstruct what had been lost, mending the wounds that had emerged in relationships during those challenging and dark periods. This collective effort marked a significant chapter in the city's history, symbolizing resilience and the triumph of unity over adversity.

The traces left by the devastating catastrophe were clearly visible in the landscape, reminding people of the difficult times they had gone through. However, instead of sinking into despair, humanity found in those scars a constant source of inspiration and motivation. The marks of catastrophe served as a perpetual reminder of humanity's innate ability to face adversity and emerge stronger and wiser from its challenges.

The story of Gabriel and the Leviathans, an epic tale of courage, sacrifice, and redemption, became a legend that transcended time.

This compelling tale would be woven into the fabric of history, a timeless narrative passed down from one generation to the next, akin to a guiding torch illuminating the path for those confronting similar tribulations in times to come. The chronicle of Gabriel and his dedicated team, their valiant stand against impending disaster, the challenging choices they made, and the sacrifices for the greater good, emerged as a shining beacon of hope. It served as a poignant reminder that, even amid the bleakest moments, humanity possessed the remarkable capacity to discover and embrace the light.

The legend of Gabriel and his team not only captured hearts but also stood as a testament to the remarkable influence individual actions could wield on the collective destiny.

Their unwavering courage and unyielding determination served as a powerful illustration that, even when confronted with seemingly insurmountable challenges, a small group of individuals had the capacity to alter the course of history. Their actions became a crucial catalyst in the restoration of a world marred by adversity.

 The legacy of Gabriel and the Leviathans was not only kept alive in the stories being told throughout the generations, but also became a call to action for people around the world.

This legend reminded everyone that no matter how daunting the circumstances, they had within them the strength and determination to overcome any obstacle.

Thus, the scars of the catastrophe not only marked the past, but also became symbols of resilience, hope and humanity's eternal ability to learn from its mistakes and move towards a better future. In a restored world, the scars reminiscent of the dark past served as reminders of the strength and determination that existed in the human heart.

The enduring legacy of Gabriel and the Leviathans served as a beacon of hope, assuring humanity that in the face of challenges, there would always be a path to triumph and the creation of a new chapter in Earth's history.

The residents of Aerópolis held the Leviathans in high regard, recognizing them as heroes who made the ultimate sacrifice to safeguard humanity. To immortalize their bravery and pivotal role in Earth's restoration, a majestic monument was planned, set to stand as an eternal reminder for generations to come.

Aerópolis, the once-devastated floating city, transformed into a symbol of hope in a healed world. The newfound harmony between humanity and nature became a cherished aspect of life, prompting the establishment of comprehensive laws and regulations. These measures aimed to safeguard the environment, preventing a recurrence of the errors that had led to past calamities. The city stood as a testament to the collective commitment to a sustainable and responsible coexistence with the Earth.

Gabriel and his dedicated team, fueled by a sense of purpose, actively engaged in the ongoing efforts to rebuild and champion sustainability. Drawing upon their wealth of experience and understanding, they took on the responsibility of educating the population about the critical significance of tending to the natural world and fostering a harmonious existence with the Earth. Their unwavering commitment served as a beacon, igniting a collective passion that motivated others to join the cause, fostering a collaborative spirit aimed at ensuring a more vibrant and sustainable future.

The tale of Gabriel and the Leviathans was destined to be recounted to future generations, weaving a narrative that evoked admiration and respect. The legend of Aerópolis emerged as a wellspring of inspiration, illustrating the undeniable truth that even amidst the bleakest moments, humanity possessed the resilience to discover light and redemption.

The restored world was thriving, and Aeropolis, with its story of courage and determination, was leading the way toward a future in which humanity lived in harmony with nature. The floating city had become a beacon of hope, a constant reminder that, despite the challenges, there was always the possibility of a better tomorrow.

# Chapter 19
# The Guardians of the Ocean

In the ongoing rejuvenation of Earth, the Leviathans seamlessly transitioned into the revered guardians of the seas, attaining a mythical status akin to deities. Regarded as eternal protectors residing in the ocean's depths, their tales and remarkable deeds became a cherished oral tradition, handed down with care from one generation to the next. The enduring legacy of the Leviathans emerged as a potent emblem of hope, embodying the resilience of life and the promise of a revitalized world.

In the heart of Aeropolis and the neighboring communities, a cherished tradition took root—an annual celebration paying  homage to the Leviathans. These joyous yet solemn festivals were a testament to the sea creatures' vital contribution in Earth's restoration. Year after year, the community eagerly anticipated these vibrant gatherings, coming together to commemorate and express gratitude for the Leviathans' profound sacrifice. The festivals evolved into significant events, serving as heartfelt occasions where the community united to honor the majestic beings.

The annual ceremonies were not only occasions for reflection and gratitude, but also for celebration and joy.The tales of bravery and heroism echoed through the community, woven into the fabric of everyday life.

 Elders and parents eagerly shared these stories with the younger generation, ensuring that the invaluable lessons of sacrifice, courage, and unity, learned from the Leviathans, were passed down through the ages. From early childhood, children were immersed in these narratives, instilling in them a deep understanding of the significance of cooperation and profound respect for the natural world. The storytelling sessions became cherished traditions, fostering a sense of connection between generations and a shared commitment to preserving the lessons learned from the Leviathans for the years to come.

Gratitude to the Leviathans was expressed not only through words, but also through art. Artistic depictions of these creatures adorned the walls of houses and public squares.

Paintings, sculptures, and murals reminded everyone of the majesty of the sea guardians and served as constant reminders of the debt humanity owed them.

The yearly tradition of paying homage to the Leviathans evolved into a cornerstone of daily life in both Aerópolis and the neighboring communities. These lively festivals and celebrations weren't merely expressions of thankfulness; they stood as enduring reminders of the virtues of bravery, selflessness, and working together that had empowered humanity to navigate challenging periods and construct a more promising tomorrow in a renewed world. The festivities became more than just events; they became threads woven into the cultural tapestry, reinforcing a collective commitment to upholding the profound lessons derived from the Leviathans.

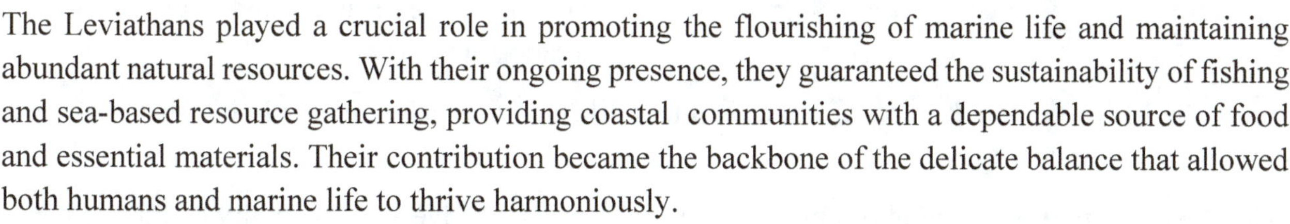

With the passage of time, the recovery of the seas became more evident and tangible. Leviathans, in their new role as guardians of the oceans, proved essential to maintaining balance in marine ecosystems.

The Leviathans played a crucial role in promoting the flourishing of marine life and maintaining abundant natural resources. With their ongoing presence, they guaranteed the sustainability of fishing and sea-based resource gathering, providing coastal communities with a dependable source of food and essential materials. Their contribution became the backbone of the delicate balance that allowed both humans and marine life to thrive harmoniously.

Humanity, having experienced firsthand the consequences of ecological devastation, had pledged to care for and preserve the oceans. They recognized the importance of these vast bodies of water as a fundamental part of life on Earth. The lessons learned through the catastrophe had led them to adopt responsible fishing practices and implement conservation measures to protect marine life and aquatic habitats. This ensured that harmony and sustainability in the oceans were maintained, which benefited humanity and the Earth as a whole.

The valuable lessons that emerged from the conspiracy and catastrophe had left a lasting mark on society.

The idea of living in harmony with nature had become of great importance. People had learned the lesson that they had to take care of their environment and natural resources. Strict regulations had been put in place to prevent natural resources from being overexploited, recognizing the importance of preserving the ecological balance.

The restoration of the Earth had become a constant commitment. People worked tirelessly to maintain the health of the Earth and were committed to living in harmony with their environment.

This meant that present and future generations had to consider environmental conservation as a fundamental part of their lifestyle. They were willing to do what was necessary to protect the Earth and ensure a sustainable future for all. The catastrophe had been a stark reminder, but also a catalyst for positive change.

Future generations, who were the descendants of Gabriel and his team, kept alive the legacy they had been left behind. They continued to promote the importance of sustainability and nature conservation. The teachings of courage, sacrifice, and redemption remained central values in the education and way of life of generations to come.

Aeropolis had become a beacon of hope for the world and a concrete example of what unity and determination could achieve.

 The floating city was a symbol of how, despite challenges and adversity, humanity could overcome seemingly insurmountable obstacles and build a better future. Inspired by the story of Gabriel and the Leviathans, people everywhere looked to Aeropolis as a role model, a reminder that nature preservation and global cooperation were keys to survival and success in a changing world.

Over the years, the communities living in the vicinity of Aerópolis experienced significant growth and prosperity.


The floating city became an epicenter of cultural exchange and  knowledge, where people from diverse backgrounds shared their experiences and learnings. Science and technology advanced constantly, but always under the motto of maintaining harmony with nature. The inhabitants of the region had internalized the importance of respecting and valuing the natural world around them. It was a deep understanding that their very survival was inextricably linked to the preservation of that delicate balance between humanity and the environment.

These lessons of respect and appreciation for nature were passed down from generation to generation, keeping the legacy of Gabriel and the Leviathans alive.

The legacy of the Leviathans was not only kept alive in the memory of humanity, but also became an inexhaustible source of inspiration for the exploration and understanding of the mysteries hidden in the depths of the oceans.

Scientific research of the seas was elevated to a position of top priority, and generations to come devoted themselves passionately to the task of unlocking the secrets hidden in the abysses of the sea.

Gabriel's descendants and his team continued to play a leading role in this field, embarking on research missions that not only increased knowledge about Leviathans, but also shed light on their vital importance in preserving the marine ecosystem.

Their efforts allowed humanity to deepen its relationship with the ocean and discover new ways to care for and protect its waters, keeping the legacy of courage and commitment alive for generations to come.

The story of Gabriel and the Leviathans, their courage in the face of conspiracy and their tireless struggle to uncover the truth, became an enduring legacy that illustrated humanity's ability to succeed when working together toward a shared goal.

Aeropolis emerged as a shining beacon of hope in a world that had recovered and restored, a testament that, even in the bleakest of times, there was always the possibility of a brighter tomorrow. This inspiring account served as a reminder that, with determination and collaboration, humanity was capable of overcoming seemingly insurmountable challenges and building a better future, preserving the eternal lesson of courage and unity for generations to come.

The guardians of the ocean, known as the Leviathans, maintained their role as protectors of humanity from the depths of the ocean. They reminded people of the importance of caring for and respecting nature.

His legacy remained alive throughout the centuries, being a constant reminder that, no matter the obstacles and adversities, humanity could find light and redemption. He also stressed that the care and preservation of the Earth was crucial to the well-being and future of humanity.

This lesson became an enduring reminder that the connection between people and nature was critical to their survival and prosperity across generations.

# Chapter **20**
# The Uncertain Future

The story of Gabriel and his search for truth was coming to an end, but the future of Aerópolis and humanity remained uncertain. Despite the challenges overcome and the lessons learned, the road ahead of them was full of possibilities, challenges, and unanswered questions.

The restoration of the Earth was ongoing, and the effects of the sacrifice of the Leviathans were becoming more and more apparent. Seas teemed with life, ecosystems stabilized, and prosperity took hold of nature. Humanity had learned to live in harmony with its environment, valuing coexistence and sustainability.

However, challenges still lay ahead. Rebuilding the areas affected by the conspiracy and battle at Aerópolis was a slow and arduous process. The emotional scars of betrayal and fighting in the streets of the floating city also required time to heal. Trust in institutions had been shaken, and society needed constant efforts to restore it.

The legacy of Gabriel and his team had become a beacon of hope and determination. Future generations looked back in admiration, inspired by the courage and unity they had shown. The stories of the Leviathans and the struggle for truth were told over and over again, reminding everyone of the importance of perseverance and the search for truth.

Aerópolis, as the years went by, became a meeting point where people from different cultures shared their knowledge and ideas. Science and technology continued to advance, but now with a focus on working in harmony with nature. Scientists and researchers devoted themselves to exploring the enigmas of the oceans, unlocking secrets that increased understanding about Leviathans and their contribution to the balance of the marine ecosystem. The floating city became a beacon of innovation and cooperation, where people collaborated to promote a more sustainable future.

The citizens of Aerópolis had internalized valuable lessons about the importance of the natural environment around them. Resource conservation and sustainability had become ingrained as fundamental pillars in their way of life.

They had come to understand that over-exploiting natural resources was a path that could not be maintained in the long term and that maintaining a balance with nature was critical to their own survival and well-being. Instead of depleting the Earth's resources, they chose to care for and protect the world that sustained them, cultivating a deep respect for the environment and its components.

The future of both Aerópolis and humanity was opening up before them, offering a horizon full of opportunities and challenges. As they overcame the aftermath of conspiracy and catastrophe, they found themselves in a renewed reality.

The coexistence between humanity and nature was appreciated more than ever, and the restoration of the Earth had become an ongoing and priority effort.

This implied that, instead of unbridled exploitation of the planet's resources, society had chosen to live in harmony with nature, caring for and protecting the world around them. This commitment to sustainability and the preservation of the Earth would influence all future decisions and actions, marking a path towards a better and more balanced future.

Despite all the lessons they had learned, questions remained unanswered. The role played by the Leviathans in the recovery of the planet raised ethical and moral dilemmas that continued to be discussed. Humanity was in a position where it had to take responsibility for protecting and maintaining the oceans, understanding that the oceans were an essential component of life on Earth. In other words, they had to ensure that the seas and their biodiversity were kept in balance, without exploiting them irresponsibly, given their vital importance to the well-being of the planet.

Society had demonstrated over time its ability to adapt and learn from the lessons of the past. The recovery of the Earth and harmonious coexistence with nature were at the heart of the agenda. Humanity had made a firm commitment to live in balance with its environment, realizing that its very survival depended on the preservation of this balance. In other words, people had assumed that they had to care for and maintain nature to ensure their long-term well-being.

As the planet recovered from past hardships, the citizens of Aerópolis looked to the future with a renewed sense of togetherness and optimism. Despite the uncertainty and difficulties that lay ahead, they were willing to tackle them with unwavering will and courage. Gabriel's story and his tireless search for the truth served as a reminder that, even in the darkest of times, there was always an opportunity for a brighter tomorrow.

The imprint left by the Leviathans and the tireless battle to uncover the truth would live on through the generations, acting as a relentless reminder of the significant perseverance and need to care for our planet. Humanity was committed to living in harmony with nature and facing the future with courage and determination, always ready to seize the opportunities and face the challenges that tomorrow would present to them. It was a deep commitment to respect the Earth and to prepare for what was to come, no matter the adversities.